SNOWGUMS TO SAND

Guide to the Port Stephens, Great Lakes, Dungog and Gloucester Region

Photography by Peter Jarver
Master of Photography AIPP

TEXT BY
Libby Buhrich
Michael Smith
Bill Dowling
Darrell Dawson
Carol Ridgeway-Bissett

PRODUCED WITH THE ASSISTANCE OF

PORT STEPHENS COUNCIL · GREAT LAKES COUNCIL · DUNGOG SHIRE · GLOUCESTER SHIRE · NSW NATIONAL PARKS & WILDLIFE SERVICE · FUJI FILMS

INTRODUCTION

Just two and a half hours north of Sydney and twenty minutes north of Newcastle lies a protected triangle of natural beauty, accessible but undisturbed by the pressures of urban life. From Port Stephens in the south up past the Myall Lakes to Forster, and from the coast inland to Barrington Tops, this triangle begins from the wild and scenic rivers at the wilderness peaks and extends to a spectacular coastline.

With a history stretching from agricultural, fishing and forestry activities to a gentle past when Koori tribes lived a free and idyllic lifestyle, the natural environment surrounds and welcomes visitors to exploration and discovery. This unique region covers diverse ecosystems, from the highest peaks of the Barringtons where snowgums grow protected by the World Heritage convention, to the stretch of wilderness coast where dolphins play and whales pass by strings of fragile lakes stretching between dunes and sea.

Barrington Tops is a world class National Park and declared wilderness area, offering walks and lookouts over ancient volcanic peaks and primeval Antarctic beech forests. The snowgums' open boughs hold wintertime snow in moving mists and sunshine, in alpine meadows close to subtropical rainforests.

Wild rivers tumble down the peaks, and then meander across green fields and winding valleys through to a lake system extending along a forty kilometre coastline. Paperbark forests fringe the water in the Myall Lakes National Park, and rainforest and heathlands offer tranquil protection and important habitat to a wide variety of birds, fish and mammals.

Port Stephens is a superb natural harbour, with the two distinctive volcanic peaks of Yacaaba and Tomaree marking the entrance. Ringing the aquamarine, crystal waters where the dolphins play, the eucalypt-covered headlands are separated by white sandy beaches and a jumble of rocky bays. A scuba diver's haven of coral, coloured fish and underwater cliffs, the marine reserve at Fly Point is listed on the National Estate for its unique sponge gardens; and west along the peninsula, the thirty-two kilometres of windblown sand dunes at Stockton Bight comprise the largest continuous mobile sand mass in New South Wales.

This book has been undertaken in a collaboration between artistic and professional excellence, statutory authorities and the local community, and it presents the fundamental essence of the natural environment in a visual essay of spectacular scenery and regional landscapes.

Let us take you there to experience the best of these natural jewels— along the local roads, past the historic villages, through the rainforest and into the wilderness to explore …

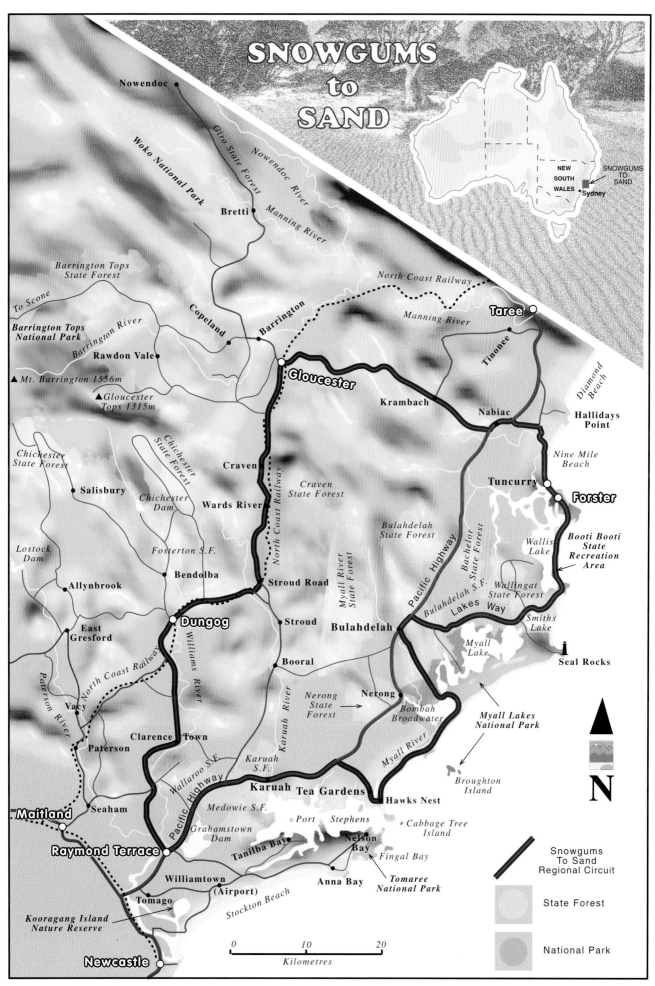

SNOWGUMS to SAND

NEW SOUTH WALES

SNOWGUMS TO SAND

Sydney

Nowendoc

Woko National Park

Giro State Forest

Nowendoc River

Bretti

Manning River

Barrington Tops State Forest

North Coast Railway

Manning River

Taree

To Scone

Copeland

Barrington

Barrington Tops National Park

Barrington River

Gloucester

Tinonee

Diamond Beach

Rawdon Vale

Krambach

Nabiac

Hallidays Point

▲ Mt. Barrington 1556m

▲ Gloucester Tops 1315m

Nine Mile Beach

Chichester State Forest

Chichester State Forest

Craven

Tuncurry

Forster

Salisbury

Chichester Dam

Wards River

Craven State Forest

Booti Booti State Recreation Area

Wallis Lake

Bachelor State Forest

Bulahdelah State Forest

Lostock Dam

Fosterton S.F.

North Coast Railway

Myall River State Forest

Bulahdelah S.F.

Smiths Lake

Allynbrook

Bendolba

Stroud Road

Pacific Highway

Lakes Way

East Gresford

Dungog

Stroud

Bulahdelah

Myall Lake

Seal Rocks

Williams' River

Booral

Karuah River

Paterson River

Vacy

North Coast Railway

Nerong State Forest

Nerong

Bombah Broadwater

Myall Lakes National Park

Clarence Town

Paterson

Wallaroo S.F.

Karuah S.F.

Myall River

Broughton Island

N

Maitland

Pacific Highway

Karuah

Tea Gardens

Hawks Nest

Seaham

Medowie S.F.

Port Stephens

Cabbage Tree Island

Raymond Terrace

Grahamstown Dam

Tanilba Bay

Nelson Bay

Fingal Bay

Snowgums To Sand Regional Circuit

Williamtown

(Airport)

Anna Bay

Tomaree National Park

State Forest

Tomago

Stockton Beach

National Park

Kooragang Island Nature Reserve

0   10   20

Kilometres

Newcastle

Clearing mist allows views northward to Tomaree Head, Boondelbah and Cabbage Tree Islands.

PORT STEPHENS
AND THE DOLPHIN COAST

ROCKY HEADLANDS

About seventy thousand years ago the sea level in this area rose sixty metres, flooding the Karuah River valley and forming the estuary of Port Stephens. The drowned valley has been described as a water wonderland. Much of the beauty is below the surface. The best place to scuba dive is off Halifax Point, where large sponges and a great diversity of marine life exist, to a depth of twenty-eight metres. Here you will meet a friendly blue groper before reaching the rocky bottom, which is covered in sea urchins.

A more sheltered dive is off Fly Point, featuring sponge gardens and coral life. One of the best shore dives in New South Wales lies protected within the 'Fly Point–Halifax Park Aquatic Reserve'. Outside Port Stephens, there are a number of other dives, the best being a swim right through Looking Glass Isle, near Broughton Island. This dive features sheer walls, schools of fish, rays, colourful sponges and the novelty of swimming right through a natural fault in the island.

Many of the boats hired in Port Stephens head straight for the tranquillity and splendid isolation of the Myall Lakes. Here houseboats, yachts, runabouts and luxury cruisers disperse to their favourite anchorage or campsite in this vast system of brackish-water lakes.

Boats choosing to ply the salt water of Port Stephens have plenty to choose from. There is carefree swimming over the sands of Shoal Bay, Winda Woppa and Dutchies Beach. It is possible to have a picnic, or a wedding on Corrie Island. Mud crabs and flathead await the fisherman in Bundabah Creek. Sea eagles and kites circle over the snug anchorage of Fame Cove. For the explorer, there are the blockhouses and gun emplacements around Tomaree, the convict-built harbour at Tahlee, the huge fig tree on Snapper Island and hectares of oyster farms in Big Swan Bay.

Migrating mullet enter the port in such numbers as to darken the water. Mackerel tuna come in from the open sea to feed on schools of small fish. Gannets, terns and gulls dive

A marine snail found on Broughton Island.

The dramatic coastline dominated by Tomaree Head stretches to the faint outline of Broughton Island.

Tomaree Headland separates the calmer waters of Port Stephens from the swells of the South Pacific Ocean.

Protected by Yacaaba and Tomaree Heads, a dolphin watch tour boat glides across the smooth waters of Port Stephens.

D'Albora Marina provides safe anchor for boats plying the waters of Port Stephens.

Shoal Bay is a popular beach during the summer months.

and swoop to pick up casualties when the tailor are feeding. Breaking the surface to breathe could be a dolphin, turtle, cormorant or fairy penguin.

Port Stephens is many things to many people. For the professional fisherman, it is a place where prawns, oysters, mullet and bream can be profitably harvested. The worker on holidays finds a tradition of accommodating the visitor while enjoying, year round, the natural beauty of Port Stephens. It is a popular holiday destination for those who love fishing, sailing and swimming in a bushland setting. Nelson Bay is the biggest town on the southern shore and is well set up to satisfy the needs of visitors. Highly productive offshore fishing grounds cater to the game fisherman, with over one thousand marlin being caught, tagged and released in the annual two week interclub fishing tournament.

In late August, a special cry can be heard from the cliffs of Tomaree. On the eastern side there is a huge gash, as if a giant axe had tried to cut the mountain in two and nearly succeeded. On an inaccessible ledge, a young peregrine falcon keeps up its begging, shrill scream. The parent is away hunting. Somewhere on the heathlands there is a galah or a honeyeater who has not taken cover. A spectacular swoop, peaking at three hundred kilometres an hour, the deadly talons make contact and another meal is ready to be shared. The swiftest of hawks, the peregrine falcon is admired the world over for its speed and audacity.

The most obvious geographic features of Port Stephens are the volcanic peaks that rise dramatically straight up from the sea to over two hundred metres. They were formed forty million years ago when molten rock flowed out of faults in the ground to become toscanite, andesite or rhyolite, depending on the minerals present and the rate of cooling. Time has weathered the softer parent rock away, leaving distinctive volcanic peaks with names such as Tomaree, Yacaaba, Stephens Peak, Glovers Hill, Kurrara Hill and Gan Gan Hill. The rest of the landscape is made up of sand, washed in from the sea, blown ashore or left behind after a fall in sea level. Some of this sand is pure silicon, and sought after by the glass industry. Others seek the heavy minerals of zircon and rutile that lie in concentrations here and there.

But, most importantly, the sand forms a base where things can grow. Firstly the grasses colonise, even where the sand is still moving. Then the wattles, tea trees and banksias further fuse the sand. Stabilised by roots and nourished by organic material, a community of plants and trees can develop. The coastal heathlands are born, and what a community it turns out to be! Angophoras, bloodwoods and blackbutt reach sufficient size and maturity to provide nesting hollows for the brushtail possum, eastern rosella and kookaburra. The nectar-rich banksias and blackboy trees feed an army of honeyeaters, noisy miners and rainbow lorikeets. Grey-headed fruit bats, known as flying foxes, visit the flowering angophoras at

night. King parrots and scaly-breasted lorikeets swarm over the blossoms of swamp mahogany. Sugar and feathertail gliders scratch the trunk for a sweet flow of sap. Magpies walk confidently across the ground to sweep the area clean of anything that wriggles. Gum leaves flutter to the ground to cap a compost of bark, seeds and dead branches. After dark, the New Holland mouse makes a meal of wattle seeds. The brown antechinus, a small native marsupial, sniffs and scratches in the litter for insects.

The final resting place of water is at sea level. Some water does not quite make it, lying about in shallow lakes, swamps and wetlands. Here, waterbirds are happy to feed on the small fish and waterplants. Dragonflies mate on the wing. Flying foxes roost in paperbarks where land predators dare not go. In the Wanda Avenue wetlands, nocturnal birds such as the rufous night heron rest the day away. In the Mambo Creek catchment, swamphens and ducks raise families on permanent or floating islands. Egrets breeding in the swamps around Seaham make use of the local grazing cattle to help flush out grasshoppers.

BEACHES

Tomaree National Park conserves over two thousand hectares of coastal bushland, including twenty kilometres of rocky coastline and beaches. One beach, Samurai, is an official nude bathing beach. Separating the beaches are volcanic hills and a jumble of rocky bays. The rhyolite rock here is very hard and the constant wave activity does little more than polish it. In many places dykes of softer dolerite intrude, resulting in the formation of chasms, pillars and caves. The coastal section from Anna Bay to Morna Point is the best place to explore these features.

There are many bushwalks to choose from. About one hundred thousand people each year walk to the top of Tomaree, 158 metres above sea level. Views extend from Seal Rocks to Newcastle. Directly below, ocean-going fishing boats pause at the base of the cliffs to catch yellowtail for bait. Whistling kites and sea eagles soar and circle around heath-covered slopes and white caps. The white cliffs of Coal Shaft Bay reflect the light on distant Broughton Island. Trawlers, cruising yachts and runabouts pass over the waters of Shoal Bay on their way to fishing grounds or distant ports.

Stephens Peak is immediately south of Tomaree. With a suggestion of twin peaks, and a seaward cleft, it mimics its bigger neighbour. There being no trees of any size, the view expands every step of the way to the top. Wildflowers here are so good as to inspire poets. Christmas bells thrive in damp patches, Gymea lilies send red spears skyward and ground orchids challenge the view for beauty.

Walks elsewhere in Tomaree National Park are mostly on fire trails. These sandy tracks lead from the clumps of pigface and coast rosemary of the rocky bays and surf beaches, to hectares of flannel flowers in the woodlands. Here the staccato chirping of the locusts is broken by the dry crunch of leaves underfoot or the 'pretty boy' call of a bird. Should these trees be swamp mahogany, then you have wandered into koala territory. These seven kilogram marsupials have 'day trees' for sleep and nesting and 'night trees' for food and socialising. Seeing them in the National Park is a possibility but a trip to the Tilligerry Peninsula almost guarantees a sighting.

DOLPHINS

The blue water off Port Stephens is part of the Pacific Ocean. Just offshore a current of water moves south at a few kilometres an hour. This southerly current brings warmer water from the tropical north. Twice a day, on the flood tide, some of this warm water is drawn into the port. High tide is a wonderful, renewing event. Clear, clean, salty water moves over the sand banks. Oyster racks are submerged. Shallow rocky creeks fill with water and become navigable. The aerial roots of mangroves disappear under the unstoppable force. Predatory fish invade the sun-warmed land.

Water need only be waist-deep to find the bottlenose dolphin fishing. Air-breathing, warm-blooded, intelligent and friendly, this fellow mammal is one of the best-loved creatures of the sea. Port Stephens has about eighty resident bottlenose dolphins. Any journey across the water usually involves a close encounter. Dolphins love to ride a boat's bow-wave. The pressure wave at the front of a boat gives them a boost. They dive, weave, kick and splash. This gives people a good chance to look at them. Dolphins are grey above and white below. If you see one that looks white it is probably swimming upside down. They do this when mating.

Man has a long association with this marine animal and there are plenty of dolphin stories. Forty years ago a local oyster farmer shot at a youthful, exuberant dolphin, which

A dolphin glides silently beneath the bow of a tour boat.

was on his lease knocking over the oyster racks. Old 'Cutfin' is still around today. You can still see one neat hole and one big chip where the two cartridges went through the dorsal fin. Bottlenose dolphins normally live thirty to forty years under good conditions. 'Nick' is another dolphin that has been around for forty-five years—still recognised by the characteristic nick on her fin. She is still breeding. Up until the 1950s fishermen would harpoon dolphins to use as bait in their crab traps. The fishermen knew that once they had killed a dolphin, none from that pod would ever come near that boat again. The boat could be painted or modified but the dolphins would never be caught by that same boat again.

That was over forty years ago. Now, we treasure our dolphins. Charter boats run regular dolphin-watching cruises. Port Stephens' dolphins are not fed or induced in any way to come to the boats. They do it out of curiosity. If they are not in the mood, they just swim away. When contact is made with the dolphins, there is always excitement. People rush to the sides and bow of the boat. The air is electric with wonder and anticipation. Most people are happy to have this small contact with a wild creature. Some want more and climb into the boom nets to be in the water with them. Some are able to touch the dolphin, others are splashed by the spray of play.

There is a place on the southern shore of Yacaaba called 'The Boulders'. Just offshore is a big hole filled with millions of round river stones. Every day dolphins gather here at the 'Dolphin Hole' to push themselves into the pebbles and stones on the bottom. This removes the lice and other parasites on their bodies. It is a sort of community bathroom—all part of life for the Port Stephens' dolphins.

WHALES

The first whale sightings of the year occur around mid-May. Weighing forty-eight tonnes, the humpback whale should be easy to find. Determined whale-watchers, binoculars at the ready, look hopefully to sea from places such as Tomaree, Fishermans Bay and Stockton Beach. A minimum sighting would be a puff of spray jetting skyward above a dark rounded mass surrounded by breaking water. Lucky spectators will be treated to an hour of tail slapping, flipper waving and spectacular leaps out of the water. Charter boats take groups of people out into the blue waters off Port Stephens for a closer encounter. Stopping the required distance of a few hundred metres away from a whale, the boat will cut its engines if the whale approaches.

Both the humpback and the southern right whale are filter feeders. They travel north to idle away the winter in the warm waters of Queensland. Over the early winter months, about three thousand whales will pass by, with full bellies, and thoughts of a possible mate. To pass the time they sing

Port Stephens is home to about eighty dolphins and attracts numerous tourists eager for a sighting.

A close encounter with a pod of dolphins.

As if to say hello, this dolphin has surfaced right next to the M.V. Surprise, *Nelson Bay.*
PHOTO BY PENNY DAWSON.

and wave and loll about. Sometimes a whale will be seen scratching on a reef, rolling about like a friendly puppy. Every few years a whale will enter Port Stephens for a look around. News travels fast in a small town and in a short time hundreds of people will crowd the headlands to watch this special passing. It has become an increasingly frequent privilege to be able to watch the antics of this intelligent, friendly and enormous fellow traveller.

GOULD'S PETREL

Cabbage Tree Island is a kilometre off the entrance to Port Stephens. This is the only known nesting site of the Gould's petrel, one of the rarest and most secretive birds on Earth. They only visit the island for about three months of the year, starting in October. Public access is not allowed on the island.

Picture a rugged volcanic peak thrusting one hundred metres out of the water, a kilometre long and half as wide. On the western face clings a rainforest dominated by cabbage tree palms. Night approaches. Nearby Yacaaba, standing over two hundred metres out of the water, sends a shadow over the waves to darken the island. Swells roll in from the north-east to crash against the cliffs and reflect back upon themselves, doubling in height. A tide ebbs and the waters of Port Stephens flow out the heads, to confuse the seas further. When there is no light left in the sky, a grey bird, thirty centimetres long, plummets through the rainforest canopy, landing right beside its nest among the rocks and fallen palm fronds. A fat, fluffy chick, bigger than its parents, gratefully receives a regurgitated meal of fish and squid. Feeding over, the adult scrambles to the nearest cabbage tree palm which it climbs using its beak, and disappears into the night. After raising its chicks, what it does for the rest of the year is a mystery. There are three hundred breeding pairs left, safe for the moment on the John Gould Nature Reserve, Cabbage Tree Island.

BROUGHTON ISLAND

Broughton Island is a faraway place. It is always an adventure to visit. A fast boat, in good conditions, can get you to one of its sandy beaches in half an hour from Port Stephens. There are no landing facilities, so you have to get a little wet when wading ashore. Broughton is an island of sandy beaches, volcanic peaks and stunted, wind-swept vegetation. Twelve

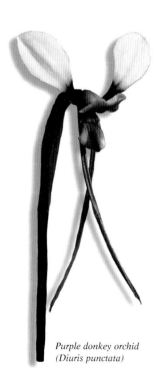

*Purple donkey orchid
(Diuris punctata)*

nautical miles from Nelson Bay, the sea journey is a kaleidoscope of sea cliffs, swells, terns, flying fish, dolphins and salt spray. Most visitors come for what lies below the water: snapper, drummer, kingfish, flathead and groper. For scuba divers there are undersea caves, coral, sponge gardens, boulders, sandy gutters, ledges, sheer walls and marine life of every type. Broughton is packed with life. In the warm months of the year thousands of shearwaters (or muttonbirds) enter their underground burrows at night, firstly to hatch and then to care for their single chick. Growing up, the young birds are left alone for long periods while their parents feed. Chicks in the nest make a lot of noise at night, like babies crying. Muttonbird parents arrive on silent wings after dark. Swooping low, they alight on the springy vegetation and run straight down the burrow. Each year they will fly up to twenty thousand kilometres around the Pacific, but, for this colony, Broughton is special. Here they were born, as were their parents and their parents and so on, for thousands of years. This island, and the food supply around it, are a vital link in the life cycle of the muttonbird.

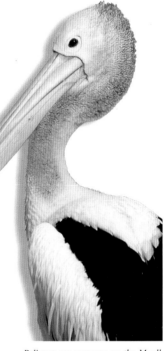

Broughton Island is part of the Myall Lakes National Park. It is essential that it stays free of predators such as dogs, cats and foxes. A torch and the willingness to walk about the island at night are all you need to observe yet another bird that breeds and sleeps underground. This island is close to the northern limit of the range of the little penguin. As soon as it is completely dark these diminutive black-and-white birds pop out of the surf and walk up the beach to their underground homes. By early summer their chicks are big and confident enough to wait outside the burrow or at the edge of the beach for the homecoming and welcome food. Adult penguins are sleek and glossy from a day's fishing, in contrast to the chicks, which resemble soft, downy footballs with a beak and flippers.

On the southern side of Broughton is a rocky isthmus known as the seagull rookery. Just after winter silver gulls lay their eggs upon the rocks, shells and pebbles. A little later in the spring, terns use the same site, laying a creamy, brown-specked egg on the ground. At any approach the birds take flight, screeching and swooping until the threat is over. Chicks and eggs are well camouflaged—this is no place for careless feet.

Rugged, wind-swept Broughton is a green oasis of safety set in a sparkling blue sea, sufficiently far from human society to preserve its timeless life cycles.

Pelicans are common on the Myall and Wallis Lakes.

THE SYGNA

The wreck of the *Sygna* lies on Stockton Beach, evidence of the strength and unpredictability of nature. The stern section of the 53,000 tonne Norwegian bulk carrier rests twenty kilometres south of Anna Bay. Standing upright and firm only 100 metres into the surf, her remains are remarkably intact considering the pounding she has received each day for over 20 years.

On the 26th of May 1974 the *Sygna* was anchored four kilometres east of the Port of Newcastle waiting to load 50,000 tonnes of coal for Europe. A gale warning had been issued and seven of the ten ships waiting off the Port had weighed anchor and moved out to sea. The wind was gusting to 165 kilometres per hour when the *Sygna* raised her anchor at 1.00am. Even with engines at full power the *Sygna* was unable to get her head into the wind. In only half an hour she had drifted sideways 11 kilometres and grounded 130 metres off the beach. As soon as the storm and the seas subsided the heavy stern settled in deeper water - breaking the ship in half. A helicopter from the Williamtown RAAF Base lifted the crew of 27 off the stricken vessel with no loss of life.

The empty bow section was dragged off the beach and sold for scrap. The *Sygna's* stern is now a popular surfing and fishing spot. Four-wheel drive vehicles can drive to the wreck from either Lavis Lane Williamtown or from the beach access point at Anna Bay.

From the hill atop Broughton Island, Yacaaba Head and Cabbage Tree Island are visible.

Water-worn rocks lay scattered on the floor of Rainbow Cave, Broughton Island.

Viewed from near the lighthouse, a huge wave crashes into Seal Rocks.

Boomerang Beach near Forster offers good surfing.

THE TILLIGERRY PENINSULA

On the south-western shores of Port Stephens lies the Tilligerry Peninsula, a quiet family destination away from the tourist bustle. Tanilba Bay greets all with its stone centenary gates, built in 1931 to commemorate the centenary of Lieutenant William Caswell's arrival in Tanilba. That same year the stone water arches, incorporating the bollards from *H.M.A.S. Sydney*, were erected to greet people arriving by water. The decorative stonework which is a feature in this area reaches its greatest whimsy in the 'Mosaic Temple of the Stork'. This contemplative structure is next to historic Tanilba House.

Christmas bell (Blandfordia grandiflora)

Mallabula and Lemon Tree Passage are the other two major towns on the Peninsula. Hemmed in by the waters of Port Stephens, Tilligerry Creek and Moffats Swamp, the Tilligerry Peninsula is almost an island. It is a unique area with its own special history, flora, fauna and attractions.

KOALAS

Enormous sand dunes are a feature of Stockton Beach, with permits available for four-wheel drives to explore the area.

A stranded paperbark tree marks time on the sands of Tilligerry Creek.

A 1986-87 survey of koalas within New South Wales identified the Port Stephens area as one of the richest koala sites in the state, and the Tilligerry Peninsula contains prime habitat which supports one of the state's last viable populations. Visitors browsing along the waterfront reserves on the peninsula may spot them in the wild, and local guides also take tours which explain the unique biology of these popular animals. Of the many eucalypt trees that grow in Australia, only a few will be suitable for koalas who will be poisoned if they eat from the wrong tree. Their favourite food trees are the swamp mahogany or forest red gum, and they absorb most of the moisture that they need in the leaves, rarely coming down from the trees to drink. Koalas are classified as "vulnerable and rare" species, and local authorities have developed a Koala Management Plan to address some of the dangers which face the koala. Being slow movers, some of the most pressing dangers to koalas include domestic dogs and speeding cars.

Port Stephens area has many suitable koala habitats, including this reserve on the Tilligerry Peninsula.

KOORANGANG NATURE RESERVE

Koorangang Nature Reserve, located in the Hunter River estuary, is one of six sites in Australia recognised by the Ramsar Convention as a wetland of international importance to migratory shorebirds. Thousands of individuals of more than twenty species of migratory shorebirds use the Hunter estuary each year. Some of the more common species are bar-tailed godwit, curlew sandpiper, eastern curlew and marsh sandpiper. These birds breed in eastern Asia, Siberia and Alaska and migrate to Australia for the Southern Hemisphere summer.

Fullerton Cove in the Hunter estuary provides a large feeding area on mudflats at low tide. However, protected places for the birds to roost at high tide have been declining over the years. The Koorangang Wetland rehabilitation project, launched in 1993, aims to rehabilitate and create fisheries and other wildlife habitat in suitable sites in the Hunter River estuary.

DUNES AT STOCKTON BEACH

South from Anna Bay lies the vast sandy expanse of Stockton Beach. A journey down this thirty-two kilometre beach is an adventure full of beauty and discovery. At the water's edge, oyster catchers, gulls and terns wait to see what the pounding surf reveals. Up on the dry sand dotterels and sandpipers groom the flotsam. Back in the dunes an ibis winkles a sand crab from a burrow, while overhead ravens scan their territory for a tasty scavenge. A fisherman reads the beach's rips, gutters and sandbanks for an informed decision on where to cast. Here and there are patches of bream, whiting, tailor and jewfish. Professional fishermen haul their catch to the beach, having surrounded travelling schools of mullet with their nets. Underfoot, pipis live in such abundance that a hand thrust into the wet sand will have one of these shellfish at the tip of each finger.

The wind-blown sand dunes of Stockton Beach comprise the largest continuous mobile sand mass in New South Wales. The yellow grains have been washed in from the sea and blown ashore to form dunes up to thirty metres high. Most of the sand was deposited about six thousand years ago. Despite the stabilising effects of plants such as spinifex, pigface and bitou bush, the wind-driven dunes move about four metres a year. The lee side of a dune is steep and loosely packed, making a perfect surface for sliding down on a sheet of cardboard or something more elaborate.

About one kilometre back from the beach, the moving dunes run abruptly into the forested dunes. At the interface, trees of all sizes are slowly covered by moving sand until they disappear completely. Perhaps ten years later, when the dune has moved on, they are uncovered to stand as stark sentinels, witness to the irresistible inevitability of sand on the march.

The dunes are a friendly place. Most plants that grow there have an edible part. Fresh water can be collected from a hole dug anywhere in low ground between the dunes. Tracks of animals and crabs lead to their underground homes and the sea is full of life. Every hundred metres, piles of bleached white shells indicate the site of an Aboriginal shell midden. These are the remains of meals eaten by the people of the Woromi Tribe and contain the bones of mammals, birds and lizards as well as the shells of molluscs and crustaceans.

As the sand moves about, it exposes sections of barbed-wire entanglements left over from World War II. The wire had been hung from several rows of star pickets along the length of the beach. Running across the beach into the farmland for several kilometres was a line of heavy concrete pyramids designed to slow down tank movements. Many of these tank traps are still where they were placed all those years ago. Some of the blocks have been moved to line the beach car park at Birubi Point.

Storms bring in all sorts of flotsam, both man-made and natural. Whole trees can be washed down flooded rivers to bob about on the high seas for a while and end up firmly embedded on the beach. Whales, dugong, fish and birds leave their earthly remains on the beach just above the high tide mark. Heavy seas or careless navigation account for shipwrecks such as those of the *Sygna*, *Uralla* and *Oimara*.

A day or annual permit allows four-wheel drive vehicles on to the beach for most of its length to enjoy the wonders of this inspiring sandy landscape.

ABORIGINAL PERSPECTIVE

Just as Australia is among the most ancient of lands (Gondwana), the first Aboriginal inhabitants (Kooris) and their culture are acknowledged as the oldest surviving culture in the world. Archaeological discoveries and modern scientific dating techniques have shown Aboriginal occupation to be around one hundred and twenty thousand years, but scientists believe the actual time is still unknown. New discoveries ensure this time frame continues to be amended.

As the world's oldest known culture, a comprehensive Koori history is still not available to us today. The information is incomplete, vague and often conflicting, having originated from poorly informed early settlers, the later work of scientists and from a fragmented oral history, culture and folklore passed on by Koori elders.

The rediscovery of their culture and the encouragement that cultural reconciliation provides has renewed the interest of indigenous and non-indigenous people in tribal language (Kattang), ceremonies, dance, art, significant and sacred places and artefacts.

Very recent discoveries of Koori habitation (campfire remains, artefacts and implements) have been dated at 14,750 years old at Medowie (1993) and at Anna Bay a

Residents stroll the washed sands of Stockton Beach at sunset.

Sunrise over Sugarloaf Bay, near Seal Rocks.

*Gymea lily
(Doryanthes
excelsa)*

large shell midden (1,240 years old) may still be seen in Fitzroy Street, Anna Bay amid the local urban settlement.

The first inhabitants of Port Stephens, the Worimi (approximately five hundred) and Wonarua peoples, led an idyllic and carefree lifestyle. The productive rivers of their territories, the hundred square kilometres of the Port Stephens estuary and the waters of the coast teemed with fish and other prized delicacies of a diverse and abundant marine life. Being hunter-gatherers, the Kooris of Port Stephens led a happy and healthy lifestyle before the arrival of Europeans; food sources were diverse and usually abundant. Excellent water sources were generally always in the vicinity.

For the Worimi coastal people, fishing, spearing, gathering, trapping, diving for food were all part of their daily lives. They were acknowledged to be of athletic and imposing stature. Their frail but serviceable bark canoes could hold two people. Freshly caught fish were usually cooked on a fire on a rock or a mound of clay and eaten immediately.

Early European writers testify to the health and serenity of their surroundings as they describe canoes on the calm, blue-green waters of Port Stephens in the early morning and late afternoon, with thin wisps of smoke rising into the still air as the fishermen patiently anticipated the approaching catch and another fresh meal. Women made the fishing lines from the bark of the young kurrajong tree. These lines were capable of landing the largest of fish.

Many native animals were tamed as pets for Koori children, who enjoyed the freedom of the natural lifestyle and were never physically punished for any misdemeanour. Music, song, dance, story-telling, and any reason for socialising, were all essential in the lives of people forever ready for fun and laughter. While each nurra (clan/sub-tribe) of the Worimi people had their own territory, they interacted, traded, socialised at corroborees and ceremonies and inter-married.

West of the Williams and Paterson Rivers, the Wonarua people hunted kangaroo and wallaby and gathered food for their daily needs, undisturbed until the intrusion of cedar cutters (1816). The early settlers then began the process of taking traditional Aboriginal land.

Their Worimi neighbours to the east had already experienced the ways of new arrivals (1790–95) and alerted the Wonarua people, who also began a long and bitter fight in defence of their traditional hunting grounds and homelands. Worimi resistance to the cedar cutters and settlers increased particularly from about 1840. 'Dawly' of the Garuagal nurra at Karuah led resistance there and was said to be 'unreconcilable' to the newcomers.

Descendants of the Wonarua and the Worimi peoples still live in Port Stephens and other areas, rebuilding their Koori identity, culture and language, and adding an intriguing and extraordinary enrichment to the peoples of all cultures there today.

TANILBA HOUSE

Tanilba Bay's first white settler was Lieutenant William Caswell, who received a grant of 50 acres in 1831 for his services to the British Admiralty. With the help of convict labourers a stone house was built. Blocks of local stone were cemented with mortar made from lime, obtained by burning oyster shells. Also used were blocks of Sydney sandstone transported as ballast in visiting ships. Features of the house include half-metre thick walls, decorative quoins that define the building edge and outline the door and window openings, high ceilings, archways and large rooms. It was a sailor's home by the water. Caswell also had a larger farm of 1,920 acres at nearby Balickera.

For fourteen years the Caswells, William, Susan and nine surviving children lived at Tanilba House. The building has had many owners in the intervening 160 years. It has been well cared for and is protected by a permanent preservation order. Sited on the shoreline of Port Stephens, surrounded by koala habitat, Tanilba House, together with its small gaol, elaborate stone gazebo and 170 year old olive tree, is open to the public.

Those lucky enough to visit the house may catch a glimpse of the resident ghost. First sighted around 1900 the ghost, a young woman with long brown hair and floor length dress, is believed to be that of Elizabeth Gray, a governess who lived there in the 1830s. She has been seen gazing through the French windows, at the doorway to the front parlour, and sitting on the end of a bed.

The locally common gymea lily puts on a splendid flowering display at Gan Gan Hill.

The Hunter Region Botanic Garden is an important repository of local plants.

PORT STEPHENS CIRCUIT DRIVE

At Raymond Terrace a sealed road to Nelson Bay passes alongside the Grahamstown Dam. Williamtown is home to dairy herds and beef cattle grazing the flats, as well as a Royal Australian Air Force Base. A turn-off at Salt Ash leads to the Tilligerry Peninsular and the towns of Mallabula, Tanilba Bay and Lemon Tree Passage. Koalas are the focus here with several signposted walking tracks leading to their habitat.

Nelson Bay is the holiday centre on the shores of the deep blue harbour of Port Stephens.

The vast waterways of Port Stephens stretch off into the sunset.

Nearby Anna Bay is the gateway to Stockton Beach, magnificent dunes, and a shipwreck of the *Sygna*. At Soldiers Point a finger of land reaches almost to the other side of Port Stephens. Fingal Bay is completely surrounded by Tomaree National Park and has a large protected beach. From the top of Gan Gan Hill, 160 metres above sea level a wonderful view unfolds of rivers radiating to the horizon, the shifting sands of Stockton and the magnificent isolation of Broughton Island.

Across Port Stephens harbour on the mouth of the Myall River, the twin towns of Hawks Nest and Tea Gardens are joined by 'The Singing Bridge'. At Hawks Nest and Tea Gardens a kilometre long sand spit joins Yacaaba to the mainland. A walking track leads to the 217 metre high volcanic peak passing through remnant rainforest. A well documented 23 kilometre bushwalk, the 'Mungo Track', starts from Hawks Nest Surf Club and ends at Mungo Brush camping area in the Myall Lakes National Park. A further 200 kilometres of walking along "The Tops to Myalls Heritage Trail", a journey from the sand to snowgums, takes approximately eleven days from here.

Tomaree Head stands sentinel to the large harbour of Port Stephens.

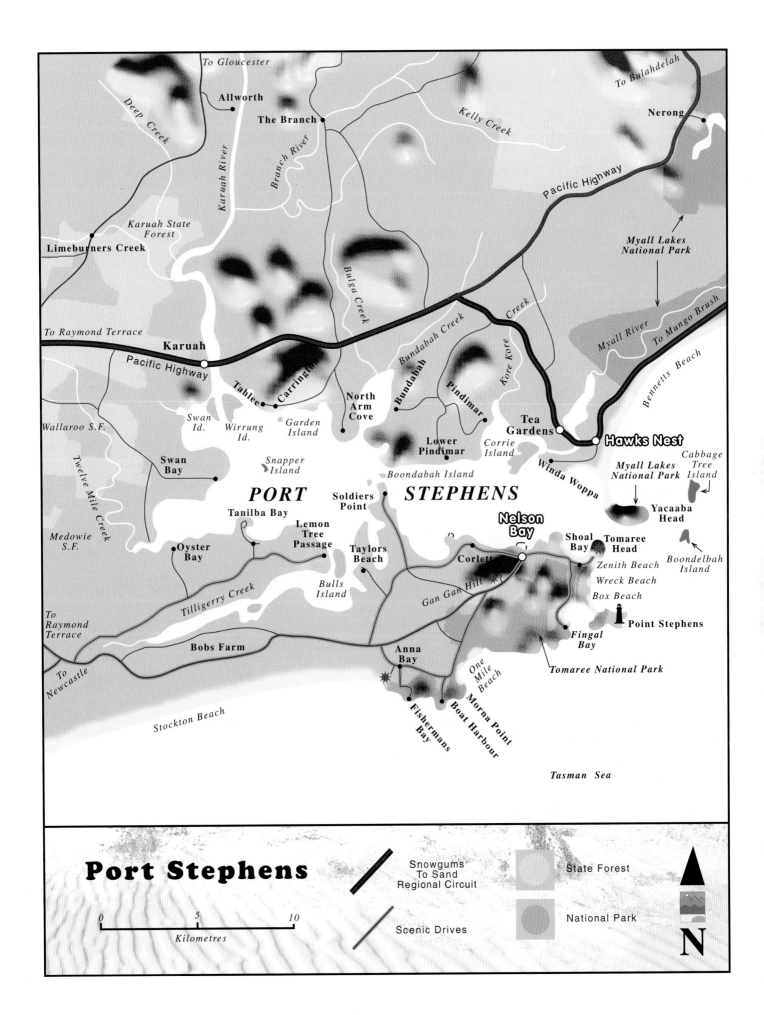

Port Stephens

To Gloucester

Allworth

The Branch

Nerong

To Bulahdelah

Deep Creek

Karuah River

Branch River

Kelly Creek

Pacific Highway

Karuah State Forest

Myall Lakes National Park

Limeburners Creek

Bulga Creek

Bundabah Creek

Kore Kore Creek

Myall River

To Mungo Brush

To Raymond Terrace

Karuah

Pacific Highway

Bennetts Beach

Tahlee

Carrington

North Arm Cove

Bundabah

Pindimar

Tea Gardens

Hawks Nest

Wallaroo S.F.

Swan Id.

Wirrung Id.

Garden Island

Lower Pindimar

Corrie Island

Cabbage Tree Island

Swan Bay

Snapper Island

Boondabah Island

Winda Woppa

Myall Lakes National Park

Yacaaba Head

PORT

STEPHENS

Twelve Mile Creek

Medowie S.F.

Tanilba Bay

Soldiers Point

Nelson Bay

Shoal Bay

Tomaree Head

Boondelbah Island

Oyster Bay

Lemon Tree Passage

Taylors Beach

Corlette

Gan Gan Hill

Zenith Beach

Wreck Beach

Box Beach

To Raymond Terrace

Tilligerry Creek

Bulls Island

Point Stephens

Fingal Bay

To Newcastle

Bobs Farm

Anna Bay

One Mile Beach

Morna Point

Tomaree National Park

Stockton Beach

Fishermans Bay

Boat Harbour

Tasman Sea

Snowgums To Sand Regional Circuit

State Forest

Scenic Drives

National Park

0   5   10

Kilometres

N

The Double Islands of Myall Lake are cleanly reflected on this exceptionally calm day.

THE GREAT LAKES

OF MYALL, SMITHS AND WALLIS

LAKES

*Native iris
(Patersonia longifolia)*

In the Great Lakes Region emerald forested hills roll down to silver lakes. Fragile slivers of land separate lakes and sea. Moist air rises from hills and capes and an abundant rainfall keeps palm forests wet and green. Lingering diffused light gives forest, lake and sea soft pastel tones. Strings of pristine pearl-coloured beaches lie between headlands flung up and tilted by ancient volcanic action.

At Cape Hawke, named by Captain Cook after an obscure eighteenth century public servant, a lookout commands a spectacular view over opalescent waters studded with sixty islands. They resemble pieces of a dishevelled jigsaw puzzle spreading into the mouths of the Wallingat, Wang Wauk, Cooloongoolook and Wallamba rivers feeding into the lake. At the foot of the cape the charming holiday town of Forster, with its beautiful frangipani trees, sprawls between lake and ocean.

The colourful fleet of local fishing boats and ocean-going trawlers berths in calm water on the other side of Cape Hawke Harbour at Tuncurry—which is Aboriginal for 'plenty of fish'. Rustic hardwood oyster leases radiate from islands as far as the eye can see in Australia's most productive oyster-farming estuary. Over two hundred licensed fishing boats operate from here, catching rock lobster, prawns and fish in the state's second most prolific fishing district.

Around the turn of the century, Tuncurry was a bustling port centred around sawmilling and shipbuilding. Steamboats and, later, paddle steamers hauled giant logs cut from luxuriant forests that flanked the rolling landscape, down creeks and rivers and across the lake where they were milled to manageable lengths. Ocean-going clippers, anchored offshore and in the harbour, waited to ply their valuable cargo to Newcastle and Sydney and on to the timber markets of the world.

Gracefully upturned limbs of paperbark trees link to form a canopy over the edge of Boolambayte Lake.

Today, pods of dolphins venture over the bar at the breakwater on the floodtide in pursuit of schools of mullet, into a much shallower lake. The Wallis is an expanse of silver water of immense beauty spared by lack of depth. The shape of the bevy of boats tied up at the boatsheds in Breckinbridge Channel awaiting tourists imply their destinations. Only shallow-draughted craft can negotiate the lake's tidal shallows, apart from a few scenic cruise boats whose skippers understand the channels with a dolphin-like sense. Oyster farmers have traditionally crafted charming flat-bottomed timber boats to suit their needs and fishermen operate their nets from sleek clinker built rowing boats equipped with outboard motors that often need to be poled off sandbars.

Wallis Lake stretches for thirty kilometres between the emerald hills of the Wallingat State Forest and a sliver of old land, swept with 'new' sands that separates the turquoise lake from the azure sea. Ruggedly beautiful headlands of volcanic origin rise between exquisite white-sand beaches washed with a rolling surf.

At Booti Booti National Park, one can walk between the two edges from sea to lake in a little more than a kilometre. A white sandy path leaves Seven Mile Beach through grey-green spinifex and meanders over a heathland patchworked in a profusion of delicate wildflowers in springtime. On the lake's edge one can sit beneath the shade of giant paperbark trees on a springy bank of clean dry seagrass, and look out across the transparent lake to Whoota Whoota, the highest hill in the Wallingat. This is a place of special mythological importance to local Aboriginal people.

On a pristine day, sunbeams reflect from the white sand through clear, shallow water to mirror the blue sky. The Wallis becomes a shimmering watery opal of turquoise, jade and purple lit with sparkling silver light. In the distance, mauve hills, the watersheds for the Wallingat, Wang Wauk, Cooloongoolook and Wallamba rivers, roll down from the old volcanoes of the Barringtons.

Reminiscent of northern Australia, this calm channel of water near Nerong is fringed by numerous water lilies.

*Matchheads
(Comesperma ericinum)*

THE MYALL LAKES

*Cape water lily
(Niymphaea capensis)*

The Myall Lakes stretch out in an ancient river basin locked in between high sand dunes on the coast and much older, flatter dunes on the west. For forty kilometres, beaches, offshore islands and the most extensive brackish lake system on the state's coastline nurture a wealth of ecological treasures. A magic series of geological events caused a diverse substrate that supports an immense range of floristic associations, from wildflower heathlands to luxurious rainforests.

The dunes cradling the lakes run parallel to the ocean and have been built up by the sea over various ice ages and fluctuating sea levels. On the coastal edge, old land continues to be washed with new sands. Between Hawks Nest and Seal Rocks moving 'aeolian' dunes change their shape near the seashore, where they become elegant mobiles, sculptured by the eye of the wind.

Owing to the landlocked nature of the lakes there is virtually no tidal flushing. Salt levels vary greatly from near saltwater at the prawning village of Tamboy—where the Myall River leads to Port Stephens from Bombah Broadwater—to almost fresh water at Bungwahl on the northern shore of Myall Lake. Extensive shallows and seagrass meadows provide important breeding and feeding areas for colonies of black swans and water birds, as well as supporting a complex association of salt and freshwater animal life. The Myall Lake system is a dynamic but extremely fragile area of precious coastal lagoons, constantly affected by fluctuating water levels due to storms, rainfall and tidal movement in the south.

At Mungo Brush an intriguing juxtaposition of wildflower heathlands, littoral rainforest, paperbark forest and dry eucalypt forest exists where ancient carboniferous sandstones are exposed in a sea of recent sands. About one hundred thousand to two hundred thousand years ago, when the sea level was higher and the coastline ran on the western side of the

From high above Bombah Broadwater, the other lakes of Myall Lakes National Park stretch north to Seal Rocks.

Sunrise is mirrored in the calm waters of Smiths Lake.

Old paperbark trees lean over the waters of Bombah Broadwater, Myall Lakes National Park.

A weary limb of an old paperbark tree rests over a solitary duck rippling the waters of Myall Lake.

The golden light of the afternoon sun paints an idyllic picture of Bombah Broadwater.

A lone kayaker glides over the mirror-like stillness of Myall Lake.

Houseboats are a popular way of exploring the vast expanse of the Myall Lakes National Park.

Myall River, Mungo Brush was an island—similar to offshore John Gould Island. Both support rainforest in soil derived from weathered sandstone, which is richer in nutrients than the surrounding, relatively recent, infertile sands.

The wide sweep of Providence Bay leads to Yacaaba Head and the waters of Port Stephens beyond.

The interlocking complexity of plant communities along the Mungo Brush track make it a haven for birdwatchers. Within a few kilometres one can walk from the silvery paperbark forests fringing the lake shore—lit up with fluffy cream cones in autumn, filled with nectar for flocks of honeyeaters—to dark, wet rainforests and open wildflower 'gardens'.

Two well documented walks of national significance leave Hawks Nest to Mungo Brush and the Barrington Tops. Excellent informative booklets describing the walks are available from visitor information centres at Tea Gardens and Forster.

Black swans

WETLANDS

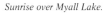

Rainbow lorikeet

Just below the lake's surface vast meadows of flowering seagrasses thrive in the light. Prawns and crabs and young fish hide from predators in nutrient-rich seagrass sanctuaries, often described as the 'nurseries of the sea'. Over thirty square kilometres of the lake's sandy bottom is covered in ribbonweed (Zostera sp.), strapweed (Posidonia sp.) and ruppia. Indeed, the lake contains the highest proportion of seagrass meadows in the state's estuaries and accounts for the rich diversity of the benthic community. Valuable saltmarsh flats found in pockets around the shores play a vital role in helping to keep the lake water clean. They act as a buffer between land and water and aid in the breakdown of pollutants.

Wallis Lake is a bird watchers' paradise. Godwits, turnstones, snipes, stilts, rakes and rails make up some of more than two hundred, often whimsically named, birds recorded here. The seagrass meadows support epiphytic algae that feed leatherjacket, blackfish and mullet, which in turn feed a startling array of beautiful birds.

A sand island close to the centre of Forster is fenced off by the National Parks and Wildlife Service. Here, the little tern, which is an endangered bird, breeds in summer after a long flight from eastern Asia. These endearing creatures remain vulnerable and threatened by predators because they lay two brown-spotted eggs in a shallow depression in the open sand.

Further south, pelicans entirely cover a sandbar known as Pelican Island. This is a nature reserve managed by the National Parks and Wildlife Service, to protect one of the most prolific pelican breeding areas on the New South Wales coast. It is interesting to watch the parent birds return to the island and disgorge krill into the fledglings' bills.

Australia's only stork, the jabiru, is a tall, stately, black-and-white bird with long red legs and a massive bill. It is sometimes glimpsed foraging around the reed bed shores or high up in a dead tree, where it roosts. Black swans feed on the vast ribbon grass meadows and the lakes' edges are always detailed with elegant giant white egrets and shy white-faced herons.

Sunrise over Myall Lake.

LITTORAL RAINFOREST

About forty-five million years ago Australia separated from Antarctica and moved northward to its present position carrying a precious cargo of Gondwanan plants and animals. As Australia drifted towards Asia, complex geological events occurred, affecting the structure of the land's surface and resulting in climatic changes. On the east coast the uplifted Great Dividing Range and the Great Escarpment, rich in nutrients from lava flows and blessed with abundant rainfall, created ideal conditions for expansive rainforests.

The east coast of Australia is the most extensive area of various rainforest types occurring in the world. Less than a quarter of the original rainforest existing in New South Wales when Europeans first settled remains today. At the turn of the century there was almost a continuous strand of littoral rainforest along the eastern seaboard. These endangered forests grow in warm moist habitats in coastal headlands or on nutrient-enriched deep sands in the lee of coastal dunes. In the past they have been vastly reduced by sandmining and the remaining rare pockets are vulnerable to inappropriate development and fire pushing back their perimeters.

ABOVE A commercial fisherman on Bombah Broadwater.

BELOW Sunrise over Mungo Beach highlights Broken Sands, Myall Lakes National Park.

Littoral rainforest occurs only on the coast and contains a large number of endemic plants as well as others represented in dry and subtropical rainforests. From the tough outer leaves facing the sun, seemingly sheared like topiary, down to the organisms recycling nutrients into the sand beneath the humus on the forest floor, they are a virtual hot house of co-dependency. Fast-growing vines quickly recolonise gaps in the canopy caused by fallen limbs, while older trees firmly buttress themselves in the moist earth and open their limbs to epiphytic ferns and heavy woody lianas.

At Cellito Beach just south of Blueys Beach, enterprising locals have built a boardwalk through an important remnant rainforest, to preserve a unique floristic association. Here you will find palms, vines and an assortment of delightful rainforest trees locked in a classic

Eastern rosella

canopy over a forest floor carpeted in wild violets and ferns, between clumps of white flowering lilies and native ginger.

There is wheelchair access to a platform close to the foot of a fascinating headland, prosaically named Bald Head. Evidence of volcanic activity can be detected with the dramatic tilt of the rocky headland. One face technically termed tessellated paving resembles a giant's staircase stepping into the turquoise sea. The headland is a magic place for a picnic, on short springy kangaroo grass studded with yellow paper daisies, overlooking the magnificent wide sweep of Sugarloaf Bay and the ruggedly beautiful coastline of Myall Lakes National Park, towards Seal Rocks to the south. It is also a wonderful place to observe wildlife—seabirds, dolphins and migratory whales.

Where the forest edge meets the beach, the vegetation forms a tight-knit rounded shape to divert upwards winds laden with sea spray. Stunted cabbage tree palms thrive in moist sand, forming part of the wind-sheared canopy. The leathery leaves of common acronychia, well adapted to retain moisture and withstand the effects of salt spray, display a characteristic shiny, round shape, flattened at the tip. This feature, common to many plants of the littoral rainforest, directs water to the forest floor and aids in maintaining humidity. It also prevents the pretty soft green liverworts and lichens, that form dappled patterns on the tree trunks, from growing on the leaves.

Littoral rainforests such as this one form important 'islands' for migratory birds. In springtime the large nomadic topknot pigeon, extensively hunted by early settlers for its culinary appeal, feeds on the new hearts of cabbage tree palms. Superb fruit doves, with their emerald wings, are difficult to see in the canopy where they forage for forest fruit. They play a vital role in the dispersal of seeds and are equipped with a large gape enabling them to swallow bulky seeds, such as those of the rose tamarind. This delightful small tree, which grows no further south than Seal Rocks, is identifiable in spring by flushes of new drooping fresh-pink leaves.

Goannas are commonly sighted around camping areas.

Two equally attractive small trees, the lilli pilli and beach acronychia, also produce an abundance of berries for the birds—both these types of berries are used for jam making and as a bush food. The lilli pilli's mauve-pink berries follow fluffy, white summer flowers. Beach acronychia, which can be found from Seal Rocks to Cape York, has small yellow flowers in autumn, followed by orange-yellow berries. Both are a favourite food of the green catbird. His intriguing cat-like 'miaow' often signals his presence in the forest before you catch a glimpse of his ancient-looking reptile-like face and bright moss-green wings, adorned with a pattern of white diamonds on his bowerbird shape.

To watch the luminous gold and blue-black regent bowerbird flit between branches feeding on the vermilion berries of the red olive berry, his golden wings glowing, lit by shafts of sunlight in the still forest, can be one of life's magic moments. It is made even more perfect by the music of whipbirds cracking and the rush and fall of waves breaking and retreating a stone's throw away, hidden behind a natural curtain of an enchanted 'garden'.

On the forest floor the bright blue berries of wild ginger are also highly sought after by bowerbirds. It is most likely the glossy blue-black satin bowerbird with violet eyes who 'steals' these berries to decorate his bower in his efforts to attract breeding partners. If there is a cacophony of twittering from tiny thornbills in the canopy, you may be about to witness the beautiful moving patterns of a diamond python slowly slithering through the tree tops. The lithe green tree snake, with big pretty eyes, is very shy. He hardly causes the fine ferns to sway as he disappears from view at lightning speed.

On the outer edge of this forest cheesewoods, tuckeroos, corkwoods and she-oaks grow in an open sunny space. Look for friendly faced yellow robins and the rufous fantail, a lovely flycatcher. A shaft of sunlight shining through his orange fan-shaped tail while he hovers in flight is a special sight. Another summer migrant, the lilac-tinged black dollarbird, may be perched high above on dead she-oak branches looking out for unsuspecting cicadas. These birds are so called because of white 'windows' seen on their wings when they roll in flight.

Other animals you may be lucky enough to see during the day include the echidna, swamp wallaby and lace monitor. At night time the littoral rainforest offers nectar and fruit to ring-tailed possums, long-nosed bandicoots, sugar gliders and a host of insect life.

SEAL ROCKS

The white lighthouse at Sugarloaf Point gleams from the rugged headland above a sleepy fishing village nestled into the hillside beside a beach strewn with boats. For over a century the lighthouse's friendly light has guided ships through treacherous seas, where a colony of seals are sometimes seen basking on offshore rocks. Below Sugarloaf Point, grey nurse sharks breed in vast caverns. Divers come from all over the world to dive in these underwater caves that are sometimes packed with up to forty grey nurse sharks and massed schools of tuna, black cod and kingfish.

Flying duck orchid (Caleana major)

In 1992, Seal Rocks was put on the world's map, when it flickered on television screens across the nation as the site of the biggest whale rescue in history. Thirty-six false killer whales were saved by hundreds of volunteers who transported them from where they had beached themselves at Lighthouse Beach to calmer waters on the other side of the cape. At Boat Beach they were guided out to freedom across Sugarloaf Bay.

Apart from the whale rescue and the ensuing annual inundation by campers pursuing a low-cost beach holiday in summertime, nothing much has changed since the 1950s in Seal Rocks. The assortment of shoebox-style cottages with butterfly roofs, mostly built by squatter fishermen from the Hunter Valley back then, still look out over Sugarloaf Bay at a coastline classified by the National Trust for its inherent rugged beauty. All but the handful of houses which are now freehold title, and some on crown land, lie in Myall Lakes National Park.

Two special subtropical rainforest walks not to be missed in the Great Lakes Region are at Bungwahl and west of Bulahdelah, conserved in State Forest.

BOOTI BOOTI NATIONAL PARK

A vast array of diverse habitats presents the ecotourist coming to the Great Lakes area with a wide range of quality experiences. At Booti Booti National Park a well established walking track climbs through an enchanting littoral rainforest from Elizabeth Beach at Charlotte Head.

Waterhen

The path crosses a contour around Booti Hill where pretty grey-pink and cream-toned trunks of grey gums spread out over kangaroo grass. This grass is aptly named after the shape of the seed head and a favourite food of the red-browed bird—a tiny beige and scarlet

SUGARLOAF POINT LIGHTHOUSE

In 1874 building contractor James McLeod began work on Sugarloaf Point Lighthouse, three lighthouse keepers cottages, outhouses, a breakwater and a road to Seal Rocks from the Myall Lakes. It took twelve months and 18,937 pounds sterling to complete the complex. On the 1st of December 1875 the Colonial Architect, James Barnet, who also designed the Sydney GPO and many other lighthouses on the New South Wales coast, arrived at Seal Rocks in the steamer *Ajax* for the final inspection before illuminating the light for the first time.

Since then twenty ships have been wrecked in the vicinity of Sugar Loaf Lighthouse and Seal Rocks. The remains of Australia's largest diveable shipwreck the S.S. *Satara* lies 42 metres on the

sea-bed off Lighthouse Beach. One hundred people on a voyage to India were saved when the *Satara* went down. Passengers on the steamer *Catterthun* bound for China were not as fortunate. Fifty-five lives were lost when the *Catterthun* sank in 1895 in one of Australia's worst shipping disasters.

Until 1960 three lighthouse keepers lived in the cottages with their families and worked alternate four hourly shifts throughout the night to keep the vaporised kerosene light alight. Today Sugarloaf Point Lighthouse, one of only two 19th century lighthouses on the Australian coast with an external spiral staircase, is protected on the Register of the National Estate.

Aerial view of Forster-Tuncurry shows Wallis Lake stretching into the distance.

Unusually low water levels reveal the intricate sand patterns of Smiths Lake.

A narrow track leads to a secluded camping site on a remote stretch of coastline near Seal Rocks.

Wax flower
(Eriostemon australasius)

finch that feeds in flocks and looks as though he is dressed in a jaunty military uniform. Look out for the common jezabel or the painted lady butterflies, two of the thirty-five species recorded in Booti Booti.

Looking out across the sand isthmus dividing sparkling Wallis Lake from the ultramarine sea, and the surf rolling onto Seven Mile beach, the views along this walk are exhilarating on a sunny blue day. The path returns in a loop through the shade of whispering casuarinas along the grassy edge of Wallis Lake.

In springtime in Booti Booti, one can leave the turquoise sea at Seven Mile Beach and walk through the pink pigface plants and grey-green spinifex growing on the edge of the dunes and face a sea of delicate wildflowers. A white sandy path leads to the lake through a treeless windswept expanse, patchworked in spring with myriads of fragile white, yellow, pink and red and blue wildflowers.

The charming pink-red, green-tipped bells of correa flower first, followed by pink wax flowers, boronias and pink swamp heath. Peppermint-white epacris and wedding bush mingle with yellow drumsticks and golden glory pea beside egg-and-bacon and delicate lemon-yellow guinea flowers. Fragile one-day-flowering purple flag irises thrive in coarse dry sand beside the path. Beacons of vermilion and gold giant Christmas bells radiate from waterlogged depressions further back from the path closer to the lake. Four years after an October bushfire on the heathlands, the creamy white flowers of the much loved flannel flowers resemble a cloak of wintertime snow. They grow in a great swathe between lake and sea and reach two metres high.

THE CARABEEN WALK

At Tallowwood Forest Park a charmed forest has escaped the axeman's might and metal. Forest giants spread their lovely limbs for orchids and great bird's-nest ferns to recline in. Lianas, as thick as children's waists, loop and twine in an ethereal green light. Strange bird calls and unfamiliar fragrances alert the senses.

Many of the beautiful trees here, over one hundred years old, escaped logging for timber because of the area's inaccessibility. Cabbage Tree Road was constructed in the 1950s. The short Carabeen Walk winds through an unforgettable experience where many of the trees, such as tulip oak and bonewood, growing in rich volcanic, basalt-derived soil, are in the southernmost extent of their territory. The walk, half an hour's drive west of Bulahdelah, is along Cabbage Tree Road in the Myall River State Forest.

Crimson bottlebrush
(Callistemon citrinus)

SUGAR CREEK FLORA RESERVE

At Sugar Creek there is a unique association of lofty 'alabaster' trunked flooded gums towering over elegant cabbage tree palms in a forest unlogged since the 1930s. Epiphytic elkhorn ferns and orchids nestle into the limbs and adorn the sides of several eucalyptii growing in a rich alluvial soil. Delicate ferns and bright green mosses light the damp forest floor.

The short walk in the Wallingat State Forest is clearly signposted at Bungwahl on the Lakes Way.

THE TRESTLE BRIDGE

The Trestle Bridge was one of 45 bridges spanning creeks and gullies supporting a light railway system that hauled logs from luxuriant forests down to the shores of the Myall Lake. At Mayers Point the timber was milled into flitches and transported by punts to markets in Newcastle and Sydney.

Horse traction started around 1890 and was superseded in 1914 when Sir Allen Taylor, whose company had a license from the Forestry Department to extract timber from the Cooloongoolook Brush, placed an order for a steam locomotive with the Climax Manufacturing Company of Philadelphia. The locomotive arrived in pieces by ship at Port Stephens and was punted on barges across the Myall Lake to Mayers Point for assembly. In a ceremony at Wootton the decorated locomotive was christened "Aleda" by

Sir Allen Taylor's wife, Lady Aleda. Bullock teams were used to haul logs, some with 3 metre girths and measuring in excess of 12 metres, to clearings beside the line where they were cut into sleepers. Timber cut from these forests was used in the construction of the Sydney Harbour Bridge and the Melbourne Docks. Timber sleepers were used in the construction of the Trans Continental Railway across the Nullarbor Plain and shipped to Hong Kong and China.

Today the Wootton Historical Railway Walk follows six kilometres of the original railway line through flooded gum regrowth in the Wang Wauk State Forest to the Trestle Bridge. Remnants of the largest timber trestle bridge, The Gorge, that stood 25 metres above the creek bed and curved into the forest for 300 metres can be seen nearby.

Pencil-straight trunks of Eucalyptus Grandis at O'Sullivans Gap.

The Grandis, reputed to be the tallest tree in NSW.

Cabbage palms form a dense stand at Mungo Brush.

The spiky shape of grass trees contrasts strongly with the softer background.

Tobwabba Arts showcases indigenous art produced in Forster.

One of the locals parked outside the Bungwahl foodstore.

GREAT LAKES CIRCUIT DRIVE

Less than half an hours drive southeast of Nabiac off the Pacific Highway, the twin towns of Tuncurry and Forster straddle the fishing boat harbour where magnificent Wallis Lake opens to the sea. Just south of Forster, along the Lakes Way, Booti Booti National Park stretches to the dramatically beautiful beaches at Pacific Palms, backed by Wallis Lake. Several well-defined walking tracks cross the park.

Half an hour's drive south of Forster, between Wallis Lake, and the Myall Lake the smallest lake—Smiths Lake—lies perched behind a sandbar on the sea. An interesting loop drive encompassing tall forest and the western shore of Wallis Lake enters the Wallingat State Forest at Bungwahl. A unique association of cabbage tree palms and flooded gum thrive in Sugar Creek Flora Reserve. At Whoota Whoota a magnificent view opens out over Wallis Lake, the coastline and west towards Barrington Tops. Just south of Bungwahl lovely lake scenery and another wonderful view from Violet Hill are found in Myall Lakes National Park along Violet Hill Road.

Buladelah is the starting point for investigating lush State Forests and the remainders of the light railway system at 'The Trestle Bridge' in the Wang Wauk State Forest. About half an hour's drive west of Buladelah in the Myall River State Forest magnificent remnant sub-tropical rainforest is conserved in Tallowood Park.

From Buladelah a road leads to the Myall Lakes National Park and the vehicular ferry at Bombah Point. At Mungo Brush walking tracks lead into a diverse array of habitats including rainforest, lakeshore paperbark forest and magnificent wildflower heathlands protected behind huge dunes beside the sea.

The township of Bungwahl hugs the shoreline of Myall Lake.

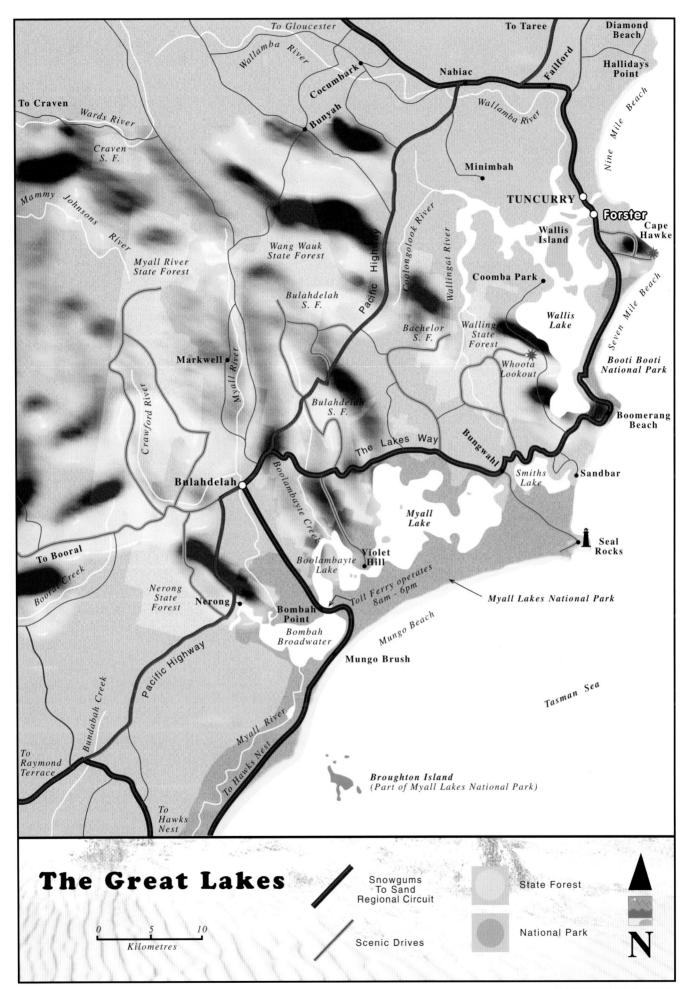

To Gloucester

Wallamba River

Cocumbark

Bunyah

To Craven

Wards River

Craven S. F.

Mammy Johnsons River

Myall River State Forest

Wang Wauk State Forest

Bulahdelah S. F.

Pacific Highway

Coolongolook River

Wallingat River

To Taree

Nabiac

Failford

Diamond Beach

Hallidays Point

Wallamba River

Nine Mile Beach

Minimbah

TUNCURRY

Forster

Cape Hawke

Wallis Island

Coomba Park

Wallis Lake

Seven Mile Beach

Markwell

Myall River

Crawford River

Bachelor S. F.

Walling State Forest

Whoota Lookout

Booti Booti National Park

Bulahdelah S. F.

Bulahdelah

Boolambayte Creek

The Lakes Way

Bungwahl

Boomerang Beach

Smiths Lake

Sandbar

To Booral

Booral Creek

Nerong State Forest

Nerong

Boolambayte Lake

Bombah Point

Myall Lake

Violet Hill

Seal Rocks

Bundabah Creek

Pacific Highway

Bombah Broadwater

Mungo Brush

Toll Ferry operates 8am - 6pm

Mungo Beach

Myall Lakes National Park

To Raymond Terrace

Myall River

To Hawks Nest

To Hawks Nest

Tasman Sea

Broughton Island
(Part of Myall Lakes National Park)

The Great Lakes

Snowgums To Sand Regional Circuit

Scenic Drives

State Forest

National Park

N

0   5   10
Kilometres

Most years, the higher peaks of the Barrington Tops are dusted with snow, although skiing is not possible on the heavily forested tops.

BARRINGTON TOPS

A WORLD HERITAGE NATIONAL PARK

BARRINGTON TOPS

Barrington Tops is a twenty-five kilometre long plateau extending between a series of extinct volcanic peaks in the Mount Royal Ranges, an easterly offshoot of the Great Escarpment. Eighty kilometres west of surf and sand, as the black cockatoo flies, one and a half kilometre high mountains rise to swirling mists. On a plateau stretched between their summits, alpine meadows awash with fragile wildflowers in springtime spread out beneath snowgums' open boughs. Melted snow becomes lithe white water dancing down to the sea through ancient beech forests bathed in an ethereal green light. Pure clear water flows from sphagnum moss swamps that retain and slowly release great quantities of water from the plateau, fed by mists, melting snow and an annual rainfall exceeding fifteen hundred millimetres.

More than twenty valleys radiate from the hub of the plateau. Wild rivers become waterfalls plunging from great heights into fern-lined gorges. In the river valleys of the lowlands, weathered basalt washed down from the mountains forms rich alluvial soils. Rainforest in Barrington Tops National Park is the southernmost link in a chain of remnant rainforests in central Eastern Australia protected by World Heritage listing. Antarctic beech forests cloaking the slopes above the nine hundred metre mark are a living link with the supercontinent of Gondwanaland, where they evolved sixty-six million years ago. Pollen of the genus Nothofagus dates back to the Late Cretaceous period, when Australia was still part of Gondwanaland. It is believed the genus evolved after links between Africa and South America were severed. Today, it is found in the mountains of New Guinea, New Caledonia, New Zealand and southern South America and relic rainforest in Tasmania. Nothofagus is the southern hemisphere's representative of the European beech.

The first stage of the Barrington Tops National Park was dedicated in 1969 with additions being made in 1982. The park gained World Heritage Listing in 1986 and, more recently, much of the area has been declared Wilderness. The pure quality of their water and

King parrot

Stately treeferns (Dicksonia antarctica) line the Honeysuckle Walk, which is a feature of Barrington Tops State Forest.

their special aesthetic beauty have enabled Boonabilla Creek and the Paterson, Williams, Chichester and Wangat rivers to be classified as Wild Rivers. Fantastic views of forested wilderness unfold from the highest peaks. On a clear day from Carey's Peak, at an elevation of 1545 metres, the white sands of Stockton Beach may be visible as a distant fine line above the rolling, agricultural, green valley of the Williams River, scooped out in a blue-green wilderness of forest. At Mount Barrington, at 1556 metres, a view to the western slopes of the Tops overlooks grazing land towards Scone in the Hunter River Valley.

At the Laurie Lookout in Gloucester Tops, it is possible to see distinct changes in forest types. Rising from the valley floor, warm-temperate rainforest species merge with wet eucalypt forest up the slopes. Where the slope retains little water, dry eucalypts thrive. Adjacent to the subalpine swamp communities and woodlands, grassy summits known as 'grassland balds' cap the summits.

The impressive array of habitats found in the Barrington Tops nurtures half of the plant species found in Australia and over one-third of its mammals and birds. A high concentration of gliders and owls, including the barking owl, which emits a blood-curdling human-like scream while hunting at night, nest in hollows in eucalypt forest that has never been logged, saved by the rugged nature of the terrain. The powerful, masked and sooty owls, however, join twenty-three other animals on the endangered list, including the tiger quoll, the red-legged pademelon, yellow-bellied glider, koala, broad-toothed rat and sphagnum frog. One of Australia's rarest birds, the tiny and elusive rufous scrub bird, may be heard singing a loud melodious song while foraging on the forest floor adjoining beech forest.

Barrington Tops is home to the magnificent iridescent blue-green paradise riflebird, which belongs to the birds of paradise family, often considered the most beautiful birds in the world. Sometimes this bird can be heard tearing rotten wood, in pursuit of insects, with his long curved beak.

While reaching up to meet enveloping mists, Antarctic Beech trees tower over an understory of treeferns.

GLOUCESTER TOPS

Gloucester Tops, a one-and-a-half hour drive over mostly gravel road from the town of Gloucester, is one of the most accessible locations in the World Heritage Area. Here you can experience the majesty of the beech forest, tread alpine paths through meadows and woodlands and watch fast-flowing streams slip over moss-lined rocks and become waterfalls.

A series of excellent walks begins at the end of Gloucester Tops Road. (For the intrepid bushwalker, Gloucester Tops is the start of a comprehensive three-day walk across 'the Tops'. After reaching Carey's Peak via the Link Trail, a return walk to Mount Barrington can be included before descending to Lagoon Pinch from Carey's Peak.) The Antarctic beech forest walk can be completed as a short loop walk among the giant beech trees, or as a longer walk following a lively mountain stream. The short walk is suitable for just about any walker of any age, and for many children it is the antithesis of what the man-made, modern world often has to offer them.

Animals you may be lucky enough to see in these subalpine woodlands include grey kangaroos, swamp wallabies, pademelons, common wombats, and red-necked wallabies. The rare and endangered eastern native cat is sometimes seen in similar habitats. Birds most commonly observed include the raucous yellow-tailed black cockatoo, the endearing scarlet robin, spotted pardalote and eastern whipbird.

WALKS FROM THE ALLYN RIVER

Several gentle day walks in Barrington Tops National Park and Chichester State Forest extend into subtropical riverine rainforest beside the classified Wild and scenic Allyn and Williams rivers, where they drop off sharply from the south easterly peaks of the Barrington Tops. The walks in the Barrington Tops National Park are near the Barrington Guest House, which has been a mecca for visitors discovering the scenic delights of forest and mountain for more than sixty years. The suspension bridges on the Twin Bridges Walk overlook the crystal waters of the Williams River rushing down the rocky riverbed through fern-lined banks. Platypuses are sometimes seen in pools beside the river bank. This walk links with the Rocky Crossing Walk.

At Chichester State Forest, the Allyn River can be

The view from Carey's Peak extends over the wilderness area of Barrington Tops National Park to Maitland and beyond.

Jerusalem Creek Falls is surrounded by lush forest in a protected area of Chichester State Forest.

The Ferntree Walk, near Barrington Guest House, crosses the Williams River by suspension bridge.

Manning Falls is a feature of the high country in Barrington Tops State Forest.

Barrington River, near Gloucester, is well known for its canoeing and kayaking.

investigated along the Allyn River Rainforest Trail. The subtropical rainforest here is well documented at twelve sites, where explanatory signs point out features of the forest which abounds with wildlife. Red cedars and strangler figs are common and the largest river oak recorded in New South Wales is here.

The difficult walk to Carey's Peak (1545 metres) begins at Lagoon Pinch, twelve kilometres by road from the Barrington Guest House. A magnificent view from The Corker rewards walkers who ascend six hundred metres in only four kilometres. The summit at Carey's Peak is a further four kilometre uphill climb.

The well documented Tops to Myalls Heritage Trail also begins at Lagoon Pinch and although the track ascends from here along The Carey's Peak Trail for approximately nine kilometres to the first campsite at Wombat Creek, the rest of the two hundred and twenty kilometre walk is generally a downhill walk. The Tops to Myalls Heritage Trail is designed to be broken up into eleven day walks, many of which can be completed as single day walks. The whole walk encompasses a wide range of ecosystems, from the alpine woodlands, subalpine meadows and beech forests of the majestic mountains at the Tops through extensive wet and dry eucalypt forests managed in State Forests in the mountains falling to the Myall Lakes. At the coast, wildflower heathlands, wet palm forests and mangrove wetlands surround sparkling lakes, heralding the walk's end, where mobile dunes meet the sea.

DRIVING THE TOPS FROM EAST TO WEST

The Gloucester-to-Scone road was originally constructed by the New South Wales State Forests for the extraction of hardwood logs. For one hundred and forty-six kilometres, the mostly gravel road provides a scenic tourist link between the Upper Hunter Valley and Gloucester, one hour's drive from the coast. Short walks to remarkable views of forested wilderness cloaking majestic mountains cross alpine meadows and woodlands close by the roadside-ideal places where less intrepid bush walkers and the very young and elderly can experience the beauty of the Barrington Tops without exertion.

After crossing the Barrington River and the village of Barrington, originally settled by Scottish families adjacent to the Australian Agricultural Company's land grant, the road

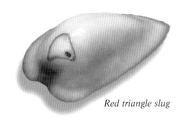

Red triangle slug

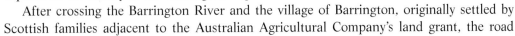

GOLDTOWN
MOUNTAIN MAID GOLD MINE

The discovery of gold in the early 1870s to the west of present day Gloucester led to the opening up of the Copeland Goldfield and the establishment of the bustling, thriving township of Copeland. During its life the Copeland field produced, at today's values, over $300 million worth of gold. For the next 20 to 30 years, up to 70 mines were being operated on the field, but this number gradually dwindled until, by 1930, only a few remained. Today, very little of Copeland Township remains to be seen. A visit to the cemetery will provide more interesting information. The ever-encroaching vegetation is once again covering the building sites, the vegetable gardens and all the other open areas. However, of those 70 mines back in the 1880s-1890s, one still remains today.

It is a working mine, and a living memory to the hard work and skills of the early miners. Situated in the valley of the Copeland Creek, surrounded by lush rainforest, including a magnificent stand of red cedars, is the Mountain Maid Gold Mine. Old mining memorabilia, including the steam engines which were used to power the stamper battery is on display. A guided walk takes you deep into the hillside, following the main shaft to where the gold-bearing ore was extracted, before it was fed into the stamper battery, to be crushed so that the gold could be separated from the quartz and other impurities. The head stamper battery still operates today, powered by a more modern method than the original steam engine.

The expansive view from Moonan Outlook will take in a distant coastline on a clear day.

Summer brings a flourish of wildflowers to the Barrington Tops.

passes by the former Copeland goldfields. At the Cobark Forest Park, a walk through magnificent stands of messmate, that has traditionally supplied timber to Hunter Valley industries, leads into an Antarctic beech forest. Moppy Lookout surveys the rugged eastern escarpment of the Barrington Tops plateau next to another short walk into a beech forest lined with luxurious soft tree-ferns.

Pheasant Creek road detour enters an unusual association of large banksias growing beneath brown barrel and attractive ribbon gum, falling away to beech forest on sheltered slopes. Where the road returns to the Barrington Tops Road, the drive rises to Polblue Swamp. Vast alpine woodlands spread out over the exposed plateau where silver-blotched ochre and cream snowgums and mountain gums thrive in wind and snow in wintertime.

A walking track around Polblue Swamp encompasses a vast sphagnum moss swamp dissected by meandering channels of icy water filled with bright green water weeds. One of the most ancient plants, the club moss grows in this maze of subalpine flora here. To the south-east, Mount Polblue rises to a height of 1575 metres in the Mount Royal Range. From Moonan Lookout, fantastic views overlook the Liverpool Range which links Barrington Tops along the Mount Royal Range to the Great Escarpment. On a clear day, the Great Dividing Range can be detected behind the headwaters of the Hunter River.

Scrub turkey

SUBALPINE SNOWGUMS

Before entering the forest, a subalpine meadow stretches into the distance, dominated by the silver-beige, ochre and pink-dappled trunks of snowgums (Eucalyptus pauciflora) glowing through soft white mist, on a moist day. In springtime, fields of bluebells (Wahlenbergia sp.) yellow and white paper daisies, (Helichrysum sp.) slender rice flowers (Pimelea ligustrina) and yellow billy buttons (Craspedia uniflora) flower between the grey-green snow grass (Poa sieberana) tussocks and strappy lomandra. Aboriginal people chewed the fleshy white end of the blade-like leaves and ground the orange seeds of this matt rush into a type of starchy flour that was easily stored. Deep blue sun orchids (Thelymitra sp.) and lovely nodding green hoods (Pterostylis sp.) can be found in springtime, flowering on slender stems below the snowgums' grey-green leaves.

Young snowgums are easily identifiable from mountain gums (Eucalyptus dairympleana), as the juvenile leaves of the latter are round and grow opposite one another along the saplings' stems.

MONKERAI BRIDGE
THE OLDEST TIMBER TRUSS BRIDGE IN NEW SOUTH WALES

During the mid-1800s the road through the picturesque Monkerai Valley provided the main road link between the villages of Dungog and Gloucester. The need for a bridge spanning the Karuah River at Monkerai to eliminate the existing ford and the associated delays experienced during times of flood was finally realised, when in 1877, a magnificent timber truss bridge was opened. Built to an "old Public Works Department" design, it has three spans, featuring flat sloping end diagonals and extra timber midspan on the upper chord.

This design was superseded by trusses developed in 1886 and 1893. Abundant supplies of hardwood timber in New South Wales led to

over 350 timber truss bridges being built between 1865 and 1915 - far more than in any other state. Today very few of these remain and Monkerai Bridge, classified as a Historic Bridge is the oldest remaining timber truss bridge in New South Wales. Other timber bridges can still be seen throughout this area, and they stand as a lasting tribute and memorial to the courage and workmanship of those bridge builders of times gone by. Sadly, these old bridges are gradually being replaced by modern steel and concrete, but hopefully, with just a little bit of tender, loving care, Monkerai Bridge will be still standing for many more years.

A distant snow shower dusts the Barrington Tops wilderness area, as viewed from Devil's Hole Lookout.

Snowgums cling to the edge of a precipice overlooking the headwaters of Moppy River.

Hardy campers endure a night of snow at Polblue, the most elevated of the camping areas.

The creek draining Polblue Swamp meanders through sphagnum moss.

BEECH FORESTS

A dramatic change occurs at the edge of the beech forest. Every surface, apart from the dark scalloped trunks of the giant beech trees and the tan, round leaves carpeting the path, appears a shade of green. Bright, light-green, thick moss glows between the lacy tracery of tree fern fronds. An ethereal greenish light shines through long blue-green, old men's beards—a long lichen 'dripping' from almost every bough, twisting high into the deep dark canopy.

The forest becomes an enchanted timeless place where children can imagine fairies among the delicate ferns and mosses clothing the forest floor in intricate miniature shapes and luxuriant textures. In springtime, the fieldia, a fragile vine with a tiny scalloped leaf, glows when it showers its gorgeous cream bells where it creeps over moss-covered rocks. Terrestrial beech orchids cascade creamy-white sprays from beech boughs. All year round, opaque putty-white elephant's foot fungi—the scale of the animal's anatomy—stands out from everything green, where it is anchored to the bulbous base of the beech. Coppice growths, upright beech tree suckers, appear here, ready to flourish if the parent tree is damaged. The beech trees also disperse seeds and many saplings can be seen emerging from the forest floor. The ingenious yellow-throated scrub wren's nest dangles from frail twigs at the end of a branch. To deter predators, this tiny designer builder, which weighs only a few grams, weaves a delicate, hanging, dome-shaped nest from moss and lichen, complete with a side door opening away from the tree, over a swift-flowing mountain stream.

Crimson rosella

DRY RAINFOREST

Two interesting areas of dry rainforest in the Barrington area are found just south of Dungog at Pilchers Mountain and north-west of Gloucester in Woko National Park on the banks of the Manning River.

At Pilchers Mountain, a curious gorge was formed when the mountain split apart. Spectacular views open out over distant Barrington Tops and into an isolated area of dry rainforest conserving large stinging trees, red cedars and rosewoods. Their boughs hold terrestrial orchids, epiphytic staghorns, elkhorns and giant bird's-nest ferns. A short walking track extends into the maze of rock pinnacles and explorable caves under huge granite boulders. The rare peregrine falcon nests in the vicinity.

HISTORIC STROUD

The township of Stroud can trace its beginning back to the late 1820s when it became the headquarters for a public funded company known as the Australian Agricultural Company. In 1824, this company received a grant of land of one million acres in an area situated between Port Stephens and the Manning River. This land was to be used for agriculture and the production of fine wool. Many fine buildings were constructed on the northern shores of Port Stephens and at Stroud. Some of these are still in use today - Stroud House, (1827-32); St Johns Church, (1833) and Quambi School House, (late 1830s). Also worthy of mention are the underground grain silos, built by the A.A. Company for the storage of grain. Many

other lovely old buildings can be seen throughout the district. Although not visited now by shipping, the river port towns of Clarencetown and Paterson still have some of their early historical buildings. Likewise, Dungog is home to many lovely buildings, some with their magnificent wrought-iron lacework still intact - a monument to the artisans of yesteryear. Throughout the countryside, at every turn, on every hilltop, can be found wonderful old homesteads, quaint country churches, many with their adjoining cemeteries and charming schools. Most of these schools are no longer in use. Unfortunately, all that remains of a number of the early buildings is a mound of rubble and fond memories.

The giant stinging tree is found in a patch of dry rainforest at Pilchers Mountain. Access is through private property and permission must be sought.

Woko National Park, thirty kilometres from Gloucester, conserves the most extensive areas of dry rainforest in New South Wales. Woko is thought to be an Aboriginal name for either the tawny frogmouth or boobook owl. The park is dominated by high escarpments and the peaks of Mount Myra, Vinegar Hill and Waikok Mountain. The park is alive with wildlife—scrub turkeys and lyrebirds are often found, scratching in the leaf litter on the forest floor. Tinkling bellbirds, satin bowerbirds, parrots, finches and wrens are common. Raptors, particularly wedge-tailed eagles, glide on wind currents down from the escarpments. Red-necked wallabies and pademelons are seen at dusk and dawn. Nocturnal koalas and quolls may be spotted by torchlight. Woko is home to the endangered brush-tailed rock wallaby, yellow-bellied glider and wompoo pigeon. Platypuses are found in pools on the river bank.

HISTORICAL ROOTS

The rolling green hills near Salisbury provide pasture for numerous dairy cows, here on their way to the milking shed.

The Gringai people of the Wanarua tribe, original inhabitants of the Allyn River district near Dungog, traditionally migrated to the Tops in summertime. Their tracks through the rainforest to their hunting grounds in the mountains were used by early timber cutters seeking red cedar, known as 'red gold'. Huge specimens, measuring up to fourteen metres at the base, were hauled by bullock teams down to local mills, or shipped down the Paterson River into the Hunter from the river port of Paterson. By 1910, a party of visitors to the Tops on their way along the Williams River to Lagoon Pinch reported only immature cedar trees.

By the 1830s, European settlers had taken up land in the rich river valleys in the foothills of the mountains and exploration of the scenic wonders of the Tops began. A few years earlier, assisted by Aboriginal guides, the first agent of the Australian Agricultural Company, Robert Dawson, visited a fertile valley west of 'The Buccons' (an Aboriginal word describing the mountainous rock formations behind Gloucester, now known as 'The Bucketts'). He was on a preliminary survey for his company, which had a land grant of a million acres between Port Stephens and the Manning River. Dawson was so impressed by the well-watered valley he found, he named it Barrington in honour of his friend, William Keppel, Viscount Barrington.

Several notable visitors to the area include the illustrious ornithologist John Gould, who visited the beautiful Allyn River district in 1840, collecting information for his eight-volume series, The Birds of Australia. A few years later the famous explorer Ludwig Leichhardt reportedly spent several nights in a hollow tree sheltering from inclement weather, on an exploration of the geology and botany around his camp at Mount Royal.

The colourful bushranger Captain Thunderbolt (Frederick Ward) started his career in crime in 1865 when he stole provisions from a dwelling near Dungog. Forty-eight kilometres of unsealed road—Thunderbolt's Way—and Ward's River commemorate him. He crossed the river on horseback in full flood. Thunderbolt's partner in crime was a part-Aboriginal Gloucester woman, Mary Ann Begg, whose prosperous father worked for the Australian Agricultural Company. After a private-school education in Sydney, Mary Ann, who was considered a great beauty, bore Thunderbolt three children in the bush. She usually wore men's suits. One of Thunderbolt's hide-outs was a cave high up in 'The Bucketts' behind Gloucester. A look-out on the Gloucester-to-Scone road also bears his name.

In 1879, the Tops were proclaimed a part of the Gloucester Gold Field after gold discoveries at Moonan Brook. Calico towns sprang up almost overnight. For seventy years, copious quantities of gold were extracted from the Copeland area, which, in its heyday, supported around seventy mines. Today, the Mountain Maid Gold Mine still operates as a tourist attraction in the Copeland Creek Valley.

Built in 1884, this historic building is now home to a bank in Dungog, the administrative centre for the Dungog Shire.

St Peters Church, Bendolba, near Dungog.

BARRINGTON CIRCUIT DRIVE

The World Heritage Area of Barrington Tops National Park can be reached from the historic towns of Dungog, Gloucester and Scone. A strenuous climb of around four hours from Lagoon Pinch, to alpine meadows, snowgum woodlands and magnificent views of forested mountain wilderness from Carey's Peak, can be reached via Dungog. Access to the start of the walk is a two hour drive along the picturesque Williams River from Dungog or the lovely Allyn River, from East Gresford, to Lagoon Pinch in the Chichester State Forest.

One and a half hours drive from Gloucester, over a winding gravel road to Gloucester Tops in Barrington Tops National Park, a three hour loop walk passes through subalpine

The classic interior of St Peters Church features three stained glass windows.

woodland and a waterfall surrounded by Antarctic Beech forest. Two hours west of Gloucester on the road to Scone, another three hour return walk leaves the spectacular view of forest and grazing land on the western side of Barrington Tops at Mount Barrington to Carey's Peak.

Dry rainforest can be found at Pilcher's Mountain, fourteen kilometres south of Dungog, in a curious gorge formed when the mountain split apart. Woko National Park on the banks of the Manning River, forty minutes drive north of Gloucester, also conserves dry rainforest and rocky escarpments.

Just north of the pretty village of East Gresford, along the Allyn River, red cedars are common. Further on, Allyn Rainforest Trail leads through subtropical rainforest.

Idyllic rural scenery and historic homesteads can be seen along Fosterton Loop Road north of Dungog. At Stroud many buildings date back to the nineteenth century and the town's association with the Australian Agricultural Company.

Golden everlasting daisy (Bracteantha bracteata)

The Moppy Walk leads one through a profusion of epiphytes, ferns and mosses, all clinging to the ancient beech forest in this enchanted section of Barrington Tops State Forest.

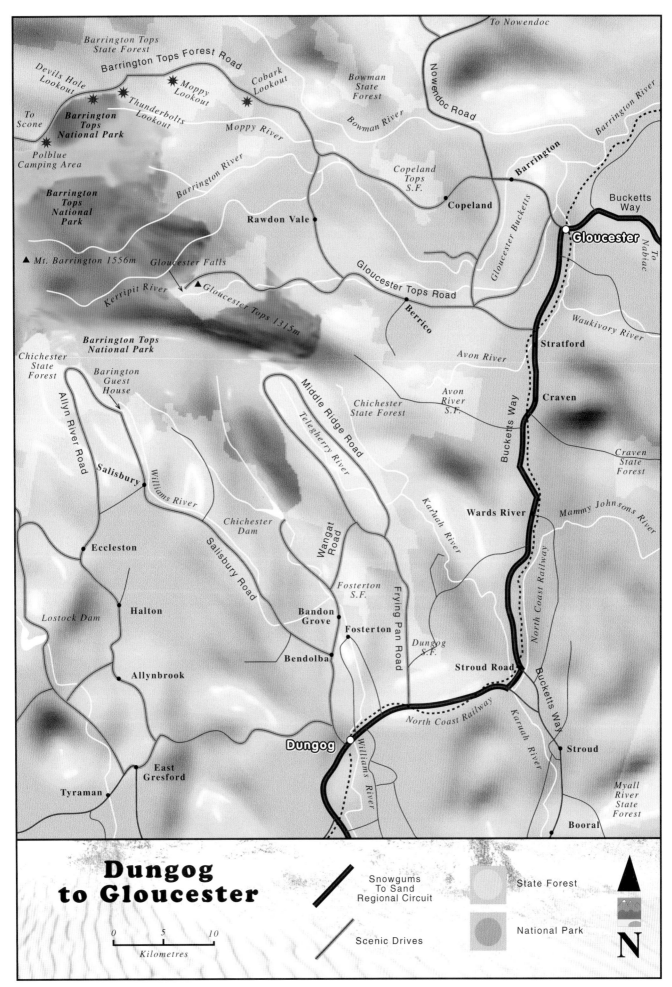

Dungog to Gloucester

Snowgums To Sand Regional Circuit

Scenic Drives

State Forest

National Park

0   5   10
Kilometres

N

GO GENTLY INTO THE WILD..

When you visit this region, make sure that you are careful of the natural environment,
and leave it as you left it. These are some of the ways you can protect it:

- Guard against any risk of fire
- Leave an area cleaner than you find it
- Be efficient with natural resources
- Stay on the trail
- Take only pictures to remember the places visited
- Be careful not to introduce exotic plants and animals
- Don't disturb wildlife or wildlife habitats
- Avoid damage to wildflowers, vegetation, earth and rock formations
- Don't use soap or detergents in natural water bodies
- Be sensitive and respect the local people
- When travelling, spend money on local enterprises
- Familiarise yourself with the local regulations
- Walk wherever possible
- Drive carefully, and stay within the speed limit

TOURISM INFORMATION CENTRES:

■ PORT STEPHENS VISITORS
INFORMATION CENTRE
Victoria Parade
PO Box 435
Nelson Bay NSW 2315
Phone: (02) 4981 1579
1 800 809 900
Fax: (02) 4984 1855

■ FORSTER VISITORS CENTRE
Little Street
PO Box 117
Forster NSW 2428
Phone: (02) 6554 8799
1 800 802 692
Fax: (02) 6555 6185

■ TEA GARDENS VISITORS CENTRE
Myall Street
Tea Gardens 2324 NSW
Phone: (02) 4997 0111

■ DUNGOG VISITOR INFORMATION CENTRE
Dowling Street
PO Box 95
Dungog NSW 2420
Phone: (02) 4992 2212
Fax: (02) 4992 2214

■ GLOUCESTER TOURIST INFORMATION CENTRE
34 King Street
PO Box 11
Gloucester NSW 2422
Phone/Fax: (02) 6558 1408

■ NPWS DISTRICT OFFICE
Lot 5 Bourke St West
PO Box 270
Raymond Terrace NSW 2324
Phone: (02) 4987 3108
Fax: (02) 4983 1031

■ NPWS TOMAREE SUB-DISTRICT OFFICE
Tomaree Crescent
Boat Harbour NSW 2316
Phone: (02) 4981 9004
Fax: (02) 4981 9012

For further information on the region
and its attractions, browse the web
at this address:
http://www.midac.com.au/snowtosand

First published by Thunderhead Publishing 1997
PO Box 549 Kuranda Qld 4872 Australia
Telephone (07) 4093 7171 Fax (07) 4093 8897
Email address: thunder@ozemail.com.au
Web Page: http://www.thunder.com.au

Photography by Peter Jarver, Master of Photography AIPP
Text written by Libby Buhrich, Michael Smith, Bill Dowling,
Darrell Dawson and Carol Ridgeway-Bissett
Dolphin photograph on page 12 by Penny Dawson
Maps by Michael Smith
Design by Liz Seymour
Separations by Graphic Skills
Printed in Hong Kong by South China Printing Co.
© Peter Jarver 1997
© Commonwealth of Australia, AUSLIG,
Australia's national mapping agency. All rights reserved.

Jarver, Peter
Snowgums to Sand
ISBN 0958906769

ACKNOWLEDGEMENTS

The Publisher would like to thank the following
people for their assistance

Mayor John Bartlett and the Councillors of Port Stephens
Dr Ted Campbell
Sarah Artist
Barrington Guest House
Junko Ichii Blades
Richard Blunt
Frank Craven
Dawson Scenic Cruises
Frank Future
Hookes Creek Rainforest Resort
Peter & Yvonne Kendall
Brian Kilby
Barbara Lane
Barry London
George Mills
Moonshadow III
NSW National Parks & Wildlife Service
Dr Jean Olley
Pro Dive Nelson Bay
State Forests of NSW
June Welsh